revolutionary

PARENTING WORKBOOK

LEADER'S EDITION

> HOW TO RAISE
SPIRITUAL CHAMPIONS

GEORGE BARNA

WITH KAREN LEE-THORP

revolutionary

PARENTING
WORKBOOK

LEADER'S EDITION

David C Cook®

transforming lives together

HOW TO GET THE MOST OUT OF THIS WORKBOOK

You can get a lot out of the *Revolutionary Parenting Workbook* by using it on your own. But you'll get even more out of it if you and your spouse work through the sessions together. Each session includes a section at the end labeled "For Couples." It will help you talk with your spouse about your responses to the session's questions and form a joint plan. Our research shows that it's infinitely better for children if parents are working from the same page.

For Couples Using This Workbook

If you and your spouse are doing this study on your own (in other words, not in a small group with other couples), we recommend that one of you work from this Leader's Edition and the other from the workbook. In addition to all of the material in the workbook, this Leader's Edition has supplementary discussion questions, along with a DVD containing five- to ten-minute videos that go with each workbook session. On the videos I share my thoughts on the topic you're discussing, and I'll also give you some suggestions as you move into the next topic. This is material you won't find in the book or the workbook, and I hope you'll find it helpful as you go through the process of making a plan for your family.

For Small Groups Using This Workbook

The workbook is ideal for a small group of parents to discuss week by week. You can offer each other fresh ideas, moral support, and prayer. If you are doing this study with a small group, we recommend that the group leader work from this Leader's Edition as explained above, and the rest of the group each have his or her own copy of the workbook. The Leader's Edition presents ideas for discussing the material in a group that are more interesting than "What did you put for question 1?" The Leader's Edition also lists key ideas for each session and offers suggestions for getting the most out of the enclosed DVD. The pages that follow give special tips and instructions for beginning your small group.

Using This Workbook with the *Revolutionary Parenting* Book

Many of the concepts in *Revolutionary Parenting* are echoed in the workbook. But we hit only the highlights here and assume you'll consult the book for the details. At the beginning of each workbook session you'll see pointers to specific chapters of the book. You'll probably want to read the book chapters before answering the workbook questions. However, if you don't have the book, you can use this workbook on its own.

GEARING UP FOR LEADING A SMALL GROUP

Using the Leader's Edition

This Leader's Edition contains the entire *Revolutionary Parenting Workbook* and more. We begin with general information that will help you prepare to guide your group more effectively over the course of the eight sessions (or nine if you include a launch meeting). It will also give you ideas on what to do at the launch meeting if you decide to have one.

You'll also notice that after each workbook session, several pages of "Leader's Guide" instructions are presented that will help you facilitate your small group. These notes include a review of the core concepts of the session, instructions on which segment of the DVD to show at a particular point each session, discussion questions, and a prayer to wrap up your group time. The "Leader's Guide" instructions are offered as suggestions; you are obviously free to modify any of this to suit the needs of your particular group.

How Often Do We Meet?

The *Revolutionary Parenting Workbook* is divided into eight sessions. The group might meet eight times, or it might meet one additional time—the launch meeting—at the beginning to share a meal, get to know each other, and hand out the workbooks.

Ideally, the group should meet weekly. Meeting every other week or once a month is an option if parents are busy, but the longer the time between sessions, the harder it will be to get to know each other well and maintain continuity.

Preparing for Each Meeting

Instruct parents to do the exercises in each workbook session *before* meeting to discuss that session. Advance prep will be important for two reasons:

- First, some exercises ask parents to interact with their children and then make notes on what they learned. Parents need to have those conversations with their children before they meet to discuss what they learned. Busy schedules sometimes make it hard for parents to sit down with their children and have important conversations, but this level of busyness is one issue the workbook asks parents to address.

- Second, some exercises ask parents to think about the uniqueness of their children and make notes about goals and ideas uniquely suited to each child. This will take a little time and thought, and each parent (or couple) will want to focus on their own children. When the group meets, parents will then have the opportunity to share what they came up with and learn from one another.

Preparation will take about an hour per session, in addition to discussions with your children at some points along the way.

Each workbook session refers to a chapter or chapters of the book *Revolutionary Parenting* for more information. It is not essential that parents read the book in order to use the workbook, but they will probably find it helpful.

As group leader, you will probably want to read the relevant book chapters before each meeting. You should also view the video segment beforehand so you know what to expect. The DVD is a valuable part of the group process. In it, I talk about key thoughts I hope you will take away from this study.

When you set up the meeting room before each meeting, check that the TV and DVD player are working and the DVD is cued up to the right segment. This preparation will avoid the embarrassment of fumbling with stubborn technology while the whole group is waiting. The most effective way to set up the chairs in your meeting room will be in a horseshoe so that group members can see one another and the TV without moving their chairs. Avoid setting up the room in rows facing the TV, as most of your time will be spent in face-to-face discussion.

Ground Rules

A few ground rules will help group members serve one another well. You will need to explain them to your group:

- *Confidentiality.* Parents will want to talk about themselves and their children with the assurance that whatever is said in the group stays in the group and is not discussed with others.

- *Openness.* Participants should be as open about their families and their feelings as they feel they can be. As trust grows, participants will become more candid. It's more important to be honest than to look good in the eyes of other participants.

- *No Advice.* Group members may share their ideas for their own children, but they should refrain from giving advice to other parents unless a parent asks for advice. Others will not be open if they fear a barrage of unwanted advice.

- *Respect.* Likewise, participants won't be open if they fear someone's critical or sarcastic tongue. It is occasionally appropriate to lovingly confront a group member about his or her words or behavior, but harshness and condescension are never appropriate. Spouses, in particular, need to treat each other with respect.

- *Preparation.* Parents should come to meetings having done the exercises for that session. A parent who consistently lacks time to prepare may benefit from hearing the ideas of others but will have less to contribute to the group. If parents find it hard to cover one session per week, the group may decide to meet every other week. Getting through the material quickly is far less important than taking time to think about each element of the planning process.

Raising children was never meant to be a solitary endeavor. We hope you find a community of fellow parents to be invaluable to your growth as a parent.

LEADER'S GUIDE TO A LAUNCH MEETING

If group members don't already know each other, holding a launch meeting the week before the first session is a great way to build rapport. Rapport leads to trust.

Consider sharing a meal or dessert, because sharing food is an age-old way of helping people to relax and feel comfortable with one another. Here are some things you might talk about over the meal or afterward:

What is your name, and what are the names and ages of your children?

If you had to describe each of your children in one or two words, what would those be?

What is one hope you have about your children?

What are some goals you have in going through this study of revolutionary parenting?

Search your hearts.... Are you really willing to change an aspect of your parenting if the Holy Spirit leads you to?

What questions do you have about the workbook process?

Make sure everyone in the group has a copy of the workbook. Make sure those who want to read the book have copies. Couples may want to share one copy of the book, but each parent should have his or her own copy of the workbook.

Go over the ground rules listed in the previous "Gearing Up" chapter. Discuss the pace at which you will cover the material. Are group members committed to making time to prepare one session per week, or will one session every two weeks fit your schedules better? Give everyone the freedom to voice concerns about time or anything else. The workbook process will uncover busyness as many parents' number one obstacle to effective parenting, but it is too complex a challenge to solve at this first meeting. It would be tragic if parents decide they are too busy to pursue a process that will help them come to terms with their busyness! If one spouse is committed to doing the preparation and the other isn't yet ready to make that commitment, you may decide to welcome both into your group with the hope that busy parents will warm to the idea of rearranging their priorities as the group goes on.

Each workbook session ends with a section titled "For Couples." Point out that section to the group. Ideally, couples will meet together to talk through the "For Couples" questions before the group meets, but they could meet afterward. Many of the questions under "For Couples" are good group discussion questions. As leader, review the "For Couples" section before each meeting to look for anything you want to discuss as a group.

Close by thanking God for each person in the group, and pray for one another as you begin to look at the way you parent.

A CRISIS IN AMERICAN PARENTING

> For more on the material covered in this session, please read chapter 1 of *Revolutionary Parenting*.

AS I'VE STUDIED AMERICAN CULTURE over the past decade, I have learned two things that should give all parents pause. First, who people become as adults—their thinking and behavior—is largely determined by what happens in their minds and hearts by age thirteen. And second, the family is one of the primary influences on that. Parents, for all the flak they take, remain one of the seminal influences in every person's life.

Yet children are in a state of crisis. Yes, many are involved in churches and youth groups. Yes, we have an array of resources for children's religious education. Yes, young people own Bibles and other religious artifacts, and they describe themselves as spiritually inclined. But let's look deeper.

First, let's look at morals. As I've studied American youth, I find that typically:

- They spend more than forty hours per week consuming media (television, movies, Internet) content.

- They accept premarital and extramarital sex as normal.

- They are desensitized to violence, having seen it thousands of time in the media.

- They are oblivious to poverty unless experiencing it themselves.

- They express a need for excessive stuff.

- They are often disrespectful and uncivil, and many use foul language routinely.

These moral weaknesses are often rooted in relational ones. Many young people shift among multiple family units because their parents are divorced or were never married. They have few role models or heroes. They find temporary bonds in constantly revolving tribes.

Many act out their relational pain through their bodies—just look at the way many use food in the twin plagues of anorexia and obesity.

Educationally, while some young people hyperperform (and are hyperstressed), basic skills are eroding for most other youth. They lack communication skills and flounder in an educational system stripped of values.

And spiritually, most are biblically illiterate and complacent. Without a coherent worldview rooted in the Bible, they cobble together assorted beliefs and are unconcerned if these beliefs conflict with each other. Most young people believe all faiths are of equal value and contain roughly the same content.

When The Barna Group surveyed eight-to twelve-year-olds about what they believe, we found that:

- Fewer than half believe religious faith is very important.

- Only one-third (36 percent) believe the Bible is totally accurate in the principles it teaches.

- Only one-fourth (28 percent) believe Satan is real, not symbolic.

- More than half believe Jesus sinned or may have sinned.

- Most believe a god exists, but only 58 percent think that God is the all-knowing, all-powerful Creator of the universe who still rules His creation.

- Fewer than one-third believe Jesus returned to physical life after His crucifixion and death.

- Only one in five reject the idea that good people can earn their way into heaven.

- Only two in five say their purpose in life is to love God with all their heart, mind, soul, and strength.

- Only one in five believe they have a responsibility to share their faith.

And the problems are not confined to preteens. We see a similar erosion of belief and commitment among today's teenagers. Thus, if who you become as an adult is pretty much determined by what happens in your mind and heart by the time you reach age thirteen, we're looking at a problem.

Yet as a nation, we tend to deny that a crisis among our kids exists. We say:

- "That's just the way things are."

- "It will work itself out."

- "Things are just different these days."

- "It's really not that bad."

- "Relax, give it time."

- "You can always find a crisis if you go looking for one."

- "It's no worse today than it was in the past."

But whether we deny it or not, the crisis exists. And who is responsible for helping kids out of that crisis? Not government. Not schools. Not churches. Not neighborhoods.

Their parents.

And when The Barna Group has interviewed parents, what have we found? Parents say they are:

- busy, stressed out, in debt

- marginally satisfied with life, marriage, job

- satisfied with *their own* parenting skills

- satisfied with *their own* children's development

- dissatisfied with the way *other parents* raise their children

- concerned about their children's *generation*

In other words, they're doing okay; the problem is with *other* parents.

Why the disconnect? The root problem is that parents have minimal standards against which to compare their own performance. Society around them has set the bar so low that parents can just about trip over it and claim victory. If their kids aren't struggling with physical or sexual abuse, aren't in gangs, aren't using drugs or alcohol, aren't pregnant or sexually out of control, and aren't worshipping Satan, they're okay. If they're eating enough, generally physically healthy, passing their school classes, and seem content with life, then they're fine.

1. Stop here and ask yourself, From where do I get my standard for measuring how well I'm doing as a parent? (Check all that apply, and add your own thoughts.)

❑   From the society I live in.

❑   From the way my family and/or friends raise and evaluate their kids.

❑   From the standards my parents set.

❑   From the media.

❑   From myself or my spouse.

❑   From the Bible.

❑   From my church.

❑   Other sources (name them):

2. What role do you think God and the Bible should have in setting the standards by which you assess your effectiveness as a parent?

8. If people are good enough, or do enough good things, they can earn their way into heaven.

_____ definitely true

_____ probably true

_____ probably false

_____ definitely false

9. My purpose in life is to love God as completely as possible.

_____ definitely true

_____ probably true

_____ probably false

_____ definitely false

10. Loving other people—including people who don't like me—is very important to me.

_____ definitely true

_____ probably true

_____ probably false

_____ definitely false

11. My faith in God is very important to me.

_____ definitely true

_____ probably true

_____ probably false

_____ definitely false

12. I have a responsibility to share my faith in God with other people.

_____ definitely true

_____ probably true

_____ probably false

_____ definitely false

This isn't the exact survey The Barna Group gave to preteens, and asking your own children isn't the same as having your children interviewed by another adult with the promise of anonymity and confidentiality, but it will give you a ballpark sense of what your children believe.

6. After you've interviewed all of your children, take some time to reflect. What did you learn about your kids?

Did you hear anything that surprised or disturbed you? If so, what?

7. To what extent do you agree or disagree that children today are in a crisis morally, relationally, physically, educationally, or spiritually? What leads you to think that?

What about your kids? To what extent do you think this crisis is affecting them?

➤

For Couples:

➤ Come together to share your answers to the above questions.

➤ In what ways do you agree in your answers to these questions? What differences do you have about these questions? (If you see things differently, practice listening to each other's views.)

➤ What did you learn from interviewing your children?

➤ What thoughts or feelings are going through your mind about this session, about your children, or about yourselves as parents?

➤ Pray together. Pray for yourselves as parents, for forgiveness in areas where you feel you fall short, for wisdom and guidance, for love for your children. Pray for each of your children, that he or she will grow up into the full stature of maturity in Christ. Here is what the apostle Paul prayed for one group of his spiritual children:

For this reason … we have not stopped praying for you and asking God to fill you with the knowledge of his will through all spiritual wisdom and understanding. And we pray this in order that you may live a life worthy of the Lord and may please him in every way: bearing fruit in every good work, growing in the knowledge of God, being strengthened with all power according to his glorious might so that you may have great endurance and patience, and joyfully giving thanks to the Father, who has qualified you to share in the inheritance of the saints in the kingdom of light. (Col. 1:9–12)

A CRISIS IN AMERICAN PARENTING

Open with a brief prayer.

Getting Started

If you didn't have a launch meeting and group members don't already know each other, give each person one to two minutes to respond to these icebreaker questions:

What is your name, and what are the names and ages of your children?

What do you hope to get out of this study of revolutionary parenting?

> As leader, you should go first with this icebreaker. (Normally the leader avoids answering questions first, but icebreakers are an exception. The leader can set an example of candidness by answering an icebreaker first.)

If you had a launch meeting or group members already know each other, open with this icebreaker:

After doing the exercises in session 1, what is one word that describes your mood as a parent right now?

Core Concepts

The core concepts we hope your group will take away from this session are:

1. Childhood is crucial. Who you become is largely determined by what happens in your mind and heart by age thirteen.

2. Parents have a huge influence in this regard.

3. Children today are in a state of crisis.

- **Morally**

- **Educationally**

- **Relationally**

- **Physically**

- **Spiritually**

4. Parents are responsible to help them out of the crisis.

5. Many parents think their own kids are doing fine, but often their standards come from unreliable sources and are too low.

You could summarize these core concepts at the beginning of your discussion, or use this as a checklist at the end to see if you covered the essential points.

DVD

View part 1 of the DVD segment for session 1. It is called "Intro."

Group Discussion

Instead of asking group members to share what they wrote for each question in the workbook, you may decide to structure your discussion with questions like these:

What is your "plan" in parenting?

How do you measure how things are going?

What role does God play in your plan?

How are your children doing morally, relationally, and spiritually? (What did you uncover from workbook questions 4–6 and the questionnaire you did with your kids?)

You may get some pushback from parents who feel their kids are doing fine, or whose children are too young to interview. It will be extremely helpful if you set an example by looking honestly at your own children and your own standards, and by sharing openly with the group what you've realized about yourself and your family.

This first discussion is your chance to set the tone for the group: Will it be a place where parents feel safe saying what they really think and feel, and what their real struggles are? Or will it be a place where parents feel pressure to look like good Christians or successful parents in the eyes of other group members? They will answer these questions by watching what you do and say.

DVD

View part 2 of the DVD for session 1 now. It is called "Review." After viewing the video, take a few minutes to discuss any questions the video raises about what your group has discussed in this lesson. Then move on to your prayer time.

Prayer

Ask, "How can the group pray for you as a parent?" Give everyone a chance to answer this question. You may need to ask some participants to be brief in order to allow time for all to ask for prayer. If people don't want to ask for prayer for themselves, you can set an example by telling the group how they can pray for you.

Pray Colossians 1:9–12 for each other. You'll find the text of it in the workbook under "For Couples."

THE GOALS OF REVOLUTIONARY PARENTS

> ➤ For more on the material covered in this session, please read the introduction and chapters 2 and 3 of *Revolutionary Parenting*.

IN OUR RESEARCH AT THE BARNA GROUP, we found three basic parenting strategies. One was parenting by default—simply following what one sees society, family, or friends do, or the expectations they loudly voice. Another was parenting by trial and error—assuming there are no absolute guidelines, some parents try something; if it doesn't work, they try something else. The goal of these two strategies is the *survival* of parents and children.

However, we also found parents who had a third strategy. They treated God's Word in the Bible as their chief source for the goals, the thinking, and the actions of parents. Their goal was nothing less than the *transformation* of their children into the image of Christ. They set the bar way above survival, and amazingly, many of them succeeded.

We identified a nationwide sample of twentysomethings who are what we call "revolutionary Christians." That is:

- God is their top priority.

- Their faith is of the highest importance to them.

- They view their world through the lens of the Bible and shape their actions accordingly.

- Their purpose in life is to love God.

- They are active in a community of faith.

We interviewed these young people about how they were raised. We interviewed their parents about what they did. And we learned an amazing amount about the type of parenting that produces a revolutionary Christian. My book *Revolutionary Parenting* is the fruit of that research.

Revolutionary Parents look to the Bible for their parenting goals. To begin to understand those goals, please read Mark 12:28–31 below.

One of the teachers of the law came and heard them debating. Noticing that Jesus had given them a good answer, he asked him, "Of all the commandments, which is the most important?"

"The most important one," answered Jesus, "is this: 'Hear, O Israel, the Lord our God, the Lord is one. Love the Lord your God with all your heart and with all your soul and with all your mind and with all your strength.' The second is this: 'Love your neighbor as yourself.' There is no commandment greater than these."

1. What does it mean to love God with all your heart, soul, mind, and strength? What thoughts, feelings, and actions does this involve?

2. Why do you think Jesus set this up as the greatest commandment?

3. Why do you suppose He added loving your neighbor as yourself as the second crucial command?

4. Imagine the people your children might be at age twenty-five. Imagine what they might be like if they become people who love God fully with heart, soul, mind, and strength, and who seek the good of others as much as they seek their own good.

How would that affect the way their use their time?

How would it affect the way they use money?

How would it affect their thoughts?

How might it affect their career choices?

On a scale of 1 to 5, how would you rate yourself on loving God with all your strength?

1 ———————— 2 ———————— 3 ———————— 4 ———————— 5

I give very little energy to
this

I invest lots of energy into
worship and God's work

What is one step you could take in loving God with your strength?

12. What have you learned from this session that will affect your goals as a parent?

In the coming sessions, you'll learn practical principles for raising children to become adults who love God and others. You'll map out a basic plan for each of your children, because every child has unique needs. You'll also assess what time and effort such a course of action will require, and you'll have a chance to count the cost for your own life.

For Couples:

> ➤ Discuss together your answers to the questions in this session.

> ➤ What do you agree on?

> ➤ How can you put those areas of agreement into practice?

> ➤ What questions or sticking points, if any, do either of you have? How can you address these?

> ➤ What help or encouragement do you need from your spouse at this stage?

> ➤ Pray Philippians 1:3–6, 9–11 for each other and for your children:

I thank my God every time I remember you. In all my prayers for all of you, I always pray with joy because of your partnership in the gospel from the first day until now, being confident of this, that he who began a good work in you will carry it on to completion until the day of Christ Jesus.…

And this is my prayer: that your love may abound more and more in knowledge and depth of insight, so that you may be able to discern what is best and may be pure and blameless until the day of Christ, filled with the fruit of righteousness that comes through Jesus Christ—to the glory and praise of God.

Pray this passage for one another as parents. Thank God for one another, for your partnership as parents seeking to live the gospel of Jesus Christ. Thank Him that He who began a good work in each of you will carry it on to completion. Pray for love that abounds in knowledge and depth of insight.

Pray this passage for your children. Pray for them to develop love that abounds in insight and discernment. Ask God to fill them with the fruit of righteousness. Thank God that He will carry to completion His work in them. Tell Him about any uncertainties you are feeling as parents.

THE GOALS OF REVOLUTIONARY PARENTS

Open with prayer.

Getting Started

Ask:

If your household had weather, what would be today's weather report? (You should go first with something brief like "sunny," "cloudy with glimpses of sunlight," or "huge thunderstorm.")

> If talkative group members start to give the details of their day, you'll need to move the discussion on gently by saying, "For now this is just a quick weather report. We can get details later when it's time to pray."

Core Concepts

1. There are three dominant parenting strategies: parenting by default, parenting by trial and error, and parenting by the Bible.

2. There are two dominant parenting goals: survival and transformation.

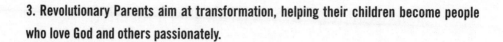

3. Revolutionary Parents aim at transformation, helping their children become people who love God and others passionately.

4. We can't effectively teach what we don't believe and live. Revolutionary Parents set an example of loving God with all their heart, soul, mind, and strength.

DVD

View part 1 of the DVD segment for session 2. It is called "Intro."

Group Discussion

If your children turned out exactly like you, would it be okay? Why or why not?

If you think of your faith as the family business, where do you want your successors to take it?

At this point, what are your goals as a parent (workbook question 12)?

How are you doing at loving God with all your heart, soul, mind, and strength? What are your strengths, and what are one or two areas where you're weak? (This relates to work-

book questions 9–11, but it's not necessary to share every detail about those questions in the group. One or two areas of weakness are enough.)

How can you grow in these areas of weakness? How can you cooperate with God in developing the habits of loving God?

You may want to underscore that sheer willpower doesn't work, especially in addressing our inner lives. There are many good resources that talk about how to work with the Holy Spirit in reshaping your desires and automatic responses to life so that you grow in love. This process is sometimes called "spiritual formation." If group members have no idea how this process works, you may want to find a book on the subject.

DVD

View part 2 of the DVD for session 2 now. It is called "Review." After viewing the video, take a few minutes to discuss any questions the video raises about what your group has discussed in this lesson. Then move on to your prayer time.

Prayer

Ask, "How can the group pray for you as a parent?"

Pray Philippians 1:3–6, 9–11 for one another as parents. (You'll find the text in the workbook under "For Couples.") Thank God for one another, for your partnership as parents seeking to live the gospel of Jesus Christ. Thank Him that He who began a good work in each of you will carry it on to completion. Pray for love that abounds in knowledge and depth of insight.

Also, pray this passage for your children. Pray for them to develop love that abounds in insight and discernment. Ask God to fill them with the fruit of righteousness. Thank God that He will carry to completion His work in them. Tell Him about any uncertainties you are feeling as parents.

BIBLICAL PRIORITIES

First Priority: God

In session 2 you looked at biblical *goals* for parents: to raise children who grow up to love God with all their heart, soul, mind, and strength, and to love their neighbors as themselves.

In this session you'll consider biblical *priorities* for parents. As Jesus said in Mark 12, God needs to be your top priority. Your children need to see that your faith in God is the driving force in your life. Your faith needs to be so central to you that it:

- dictates your life choices;

- defines your ideas of morality, success, and meaning;

- is the focal point of your conversations.

1. Read Luke 12:22–34 below, and underline statements Jesus made about priorities.

Then Jesus said to his disciples: "Therefore I tell you, do not worry about your life, what you will eat; or about your body, what you will wear. Life is more than food, and the body more than clothes. Consider the ravens: They do not sow or reap, they have no storeroom or barn; yet God feeds them. And how much more valuable you are than birds! Who of you by worrying can add a single hour to his life? Since you cannot do this very little thing, why do you worry about the rest?

"Consider how the lilies grow. They do not labor or spin. Yet I tell you, not even Solomon in all his splendor was dressed like one of these. If that is how God clothes the grass of the field, which is here today, and tomorrow is thrown into

the fire, how much more will he clothe you, O you of little faith! And do not set your heart on what you will eat or drink; do not worry about it. For the pagan world runs after all such things, and your Father knows that you need them. But seek his kingdom, and these things will be given to you as well.

"Do not be afraid, little flock, for your Father has been pleased to give you the kingdom. Sell your possessions and give to the poor. Provide purses for yourselves that will not wear out, a treasure in heaven that will not be exhausted, where no thief comes near and no moth destroys. For where your treasure is, there your heart will be also."

2. How would you summarize what Jesus says here about priorities?

In Luke 12:31 Jesus said, "seek his kingdom." In Matthew 6:33 He said, "seek *first* his kingdom and his righteousness." The thought is the same. God's kingdom, God's righteousness—God Himself and His agenda—is to be our top priority.

3. Look back at Luke 12:22–34. What are some things that Jesus said often hinder us from putting God first?

4. What about you? What would it look like in your life to make God your top priority? What actions would this involve?

5. What worries, desires, or other things interfere with your living like this?

You've looked at Mark 12:28–31 and Luke 12:22–34. Now read Luke 9:23–25:

> Then [Jesus] said to them all: "If anyone would come after me, he must deny himself and take up his cross daily and follow me. For whoever wants to save his life will lose it, but whoever loses his life for me will save it. What good is it for a man to gain the whole world, and yet lose or forfeit his very self?"

6. Based on these three passages, how might Jesus define success in life?

7. How does this view of success compare to the one our culture promotes?

This contrast between the world's and God's ideas about success is an example of the kind of outlook that Revolutionary Parents take on, live by, and impart to their children by word and example. It's a complete reorienting of priorities away from "gaining the whole world" and focusing on material needs like food and clothing, toward sacrificial love of God and neighbor.

Second Priority: Children

Revolutionary Parents' first priority is God. Their second priority is their children. Why? Serving God by loving our neighbors—or, put another way, doing the work of God's kingdom—is the second part of the Great Commandment. And our children are the neighbors God has entrusted to us in a unique way. Our neighbors across town and across the globe are important, but our children are our primary mission field. Teaching them to know, love, and serve God is our greatest act of service to Him.

> Behold, children are a gift of the Lord,
> The fruit of the womb is a reward. (Ps. 127:3 NASB)

8. Do you see your children as a gift, a reward? How do you see them?

9. How would (or how does) seeing them as a gift affect the way you interact with them?

In this passage from Deuteronomy, Moses gave God's instructions for parents:

> These are the commands, decrees and laws the Lord your God directed me to teach you to observe in the land that you are crossing the Jordan to possess, so that you, your children and their children after them may fear the Lord your God as long as you live by keeping all his decrees and commands that I give you, and so that you may enjoy long life. Hear, O Israel, and be careful to obey so

and deep is the love of Christ, and to know this love that surpasses knowledge—that you may be filled to the measure of all the fullness of God.

Now to him who is able to do immeasurably more than all we ask or imagine, according to his power that is at work within us, to him be glory in the church and in Christ Jesus throughout all generations, for ever and ever! Amen. (Eph. 3:16–21)

▶ notes

BIBLICAL PRIORITIES

Open with prayer.

Getting Started

Ask:

> Imagine you're a car. How full is your gas tank right now with physical, emotional, and spiritual fuel? (As leader, you go first. Keep this brief.)

Core Concepts

1. God must be first in the parents' lives.

2. Parenting is the parents' primary area of service to God.

3. The parent is devoted to experiencing and fostering intentional spiritual growth.

4. Parenting is a full-time undertaking.

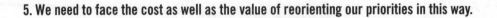

5. We need to face the cost as well as the value of reorienting our priorities in this way.

DVD

View part 1 of the DVD segment for session 3. It is called "Intro."

Group Discussion

Is your children's faith your number one priority after your own faith? Why or why not?

If yes, are you modeling faith to them? Talk about how or how not.

In what ways can you practically demonstrate faith in your family?

What worries, desires, or other things interfere with your intended priorities (workbook question 5)?

What would it cost you to put God and your children first (workbook question 14)? Why would you do this, or not do it?

Where does your spouse fit in your priorities? Your career?

Don't push parents to commit to paying the cost of changed priorities right away. Give them time to think about it without pressure as they go through the rest of this workbook. Allow them to express the emotions they likely feel when they do this cost-benefit analysis. Be open with them about what you think and feel as you weigh the costs and benefits yourself.

DVD

View part 2 of the DVD for session 3 now. It is called "Review." After viewing the video, take a few minutes to discuss any questions the video raises about what your group has discussed in this lesson. Then move on to your prayer time.

Prayer

This matter of priorities is huge for parents, and some in your group are probably struggling with it. Ask, "How can the group pray for you as a parent?"

Pray Ephesians 3:16–21 for each other and for your children.

DEVELOPING CHARACTER

> ➤ For more on the material covered in this session, please read chapter 4 of *Revolutionary Parenting*.

Now that we've looked at the goals and priorities of revolutionary parenting, let's explore some of the principles of a revolutionary parenting *strategy*.

If our goal is to raise children into adults who love God and others passionately, then our two main jobs are to *foster faith* and *instill character*. The two go hand in hand—character grows in the soil of faith—but let's talk about character first. The principles we're going to outline come from The Barna Group's interviews with Revolutionary Parents themselves. These are the things they did that they think made a difference.

Start When Your Children Are Very Young

The spiritual battle begins early. Revolutionary Parents say they started exposing their children to intentional content and experiences at age two. Seriously. You'll need to be sensitive to the stages of child development (many books on these stages are available), but key habits begin when children are toddlers. Balance the awe and joy of a new life with the challenge of shaping it. And remember: Your goal is to cooperate with the Holy Spirit in shaping each child into the image of Christ, not your own image.

If your children are already preteens or teens, don't despair. You'll get some pushback when you change well-established family patterns, but now is far better than never.

Create a Plan

You can create a plan through this simple, repetitive process: Take a first run at outlining a plan based on biblical principles and specific, measurable criteria. Implement it. Evaluate how it's going. Revise it as necessary. Implement the new plan. Continue revising and implementing as children grow and their needs change. Constantly assess how things are going and shift gears as needed.

The plan begins as you *set and pursue long- and short-term goals* (those measurable criteria mentioned above). When your children are as young as five, start setting life goals for them. Establish benchmarks in critical life dimensions, and regularly evaluate how your children have progressed and how you can help them improve their efforts. Integrate children into the process of setting goals—the process should be mutually owned, not imposed. Also, be clear in how you will hold them accountable for the standards you set together; and as they grow, increasingly involve them in planning how you'll hold them accountable.

Some of us are natural planners, while others of us prefer spontaneity. Some degree of spontaneity is important for children, because regimenting their whole lives produces rigid, uncreative, and often passive or rebellious children. But spontaneity alone rarely raises an adult with strong character who loves God and others passionately. Great parents don't reach their goal randomly or accidentally.

Every child is equally valuable in God's eyes. Yet *each child is unique, so one size doesn't fit all.* Each child requires a custom process with goals tailored to his or her needs. Revolutionary Parents notice each child's spiritual strengths and weaknesses in order to build on those strengths and address the child's needs and deficiencies.

For example, one child is boastful, with a clear sense of what he wants, a fearlessness of risk, and strong sense of his importance. His parents may set a goal for him to learn to wait his turn, to delay gratification of his desires, to grow in patience, to deal with "no" and "not yet." Another child is shy, eager to please and conform, fearful of making decisions on her own. She already understands "no," but she needs help to understand "you are loved no matter what, you are safe, you can step out in faith." The ultimate goal of Christlikeness is the same for both children, but the plan for raising them to get there—and therefore the short-term goals and strategies—will be different. The priority goal for one child is to learn patience; for the other it is courage. And in terms of strategy, these two children may need different forms and amounts of discipline. The kind of firmness the first child needs would break the second child's spirit. The second child's parents might create experiences where she will make her own decisions, while the first child's parents will seize opportunities to explain boundaries.

Each child is also unique in the speed at which he or she grows in each area of life. Our children don't need to be rushed into adulthood—they'll get there soon enough and spend the rest of their lives there. We will develop an appropriate pace as we observe our children closely and learn each one's cues.

Make Time to Talk with Your Children about Character

Teaching children about character involves both planning and spontaneity. On the one hand, *be deliberate* about planning times to talk with your children about important character traits. On the other hand, *watch for teachable moments* in which to demonstrate, refine, or reinforce those traits. Those moments come up spontaneously, and it's important to notice and take advantage of them.

Scripture identifies about forty-eight significant traits, and we found that Revolutionary Parents focused on twenty-one of those:

- Compassion
- Encouragement
- Humility
- Kindness
- Sincerity
- Perseverance
- Maturity

- Consistency
- Gentleness
- Joy
- Trustworthiness
- Self-control
- Patience
- Loyalty

- Discipline
- Honesty
- Justice
- Stability
- Reliability
- Mercy
- Love

1. Take some time to think about each of your children. How would you describe each one's personality, strengths, and weaknesses? (If you need more space than what is provided below, get some paper to write on.)

Child's name: _____ Age: _____

Personality traits *(for example, talkative, shy, likes to be the center of atten-tion, likes time alone, physically active, thinker, dreamer, doer, charmer, plans ahead, procrastinates, creative, hates structure, thrives with struc-ture, responds well to rules, needs freedom to explore and think outside the box, learns well by reading, likes pictures more than words, good listener, learns best by doing, emotional, even-tempered, easily discouraged, easily overconfident)*

Of the twenty-one character traits listed above, his or her strengths right now are:

Three character traits he or she most needs to grow in this year are:

Child's name: _____ Age: _____

Personality traits

Of the character traits listed above, his or her strengths right now are:

Three character traits he or she most needs to grow in this year are:

Child's name: _____ Age: _____

Personality traits

Of the character traits listed above, his or her strengths right now are:

Provide Structure

A fourth principle of character development is to *provide structure*. Most kids hate rules, duties, and standards, but those are crucial for shaping their character, mind, and spirit. Help them see themselves in multiple dimensions (as your child, as a member of your extended family, as a student, as Jesus' disciple, as a member of your church, as part of your neighborhood, as a citizen, and so on), and their place in the kingdom of God.

Consider the effects of your choices about rules and duties, or the lack thereof: Do they provide your children with stability, security, reliability, meaning? Or do they overcontrol (making you feel secure, but keeping children from growing up) or underguide (leaving kids to navigate the maze of life by trial and error)?

5. What roles (such as attending church each week, spending time with extended family, being home for family dinners) or household tasks (such as cleaning their room or taking out the trash) do your children know they're expected to do consistently?

6. If it has been hard for you to establish this kind of a consistent structure that lets your children know what's expected of them, talk about what hinders you from doing that.

7. The following are things Revolutionary Parents told us they did to create an environment of stability. Which of them do you want to add to your parenting plan?

❏ Tell your children explicitly that you and your spouse are in your marriage for the long haul.

❏ Demonstrate that you and your spouse are committed to each other.

❏ Establish consistent household rules.

❏ Establish clear moral expectations.

❏ Establish clear household financial priorities.

❏ Show you keep your promises by following through on rules and expectations you've established, as well as consistent consequences if children break the rules.

❏ Talk about and live by a consistent philosophy of life.

8. If you're a single parent, you already know the challenges of not having a partner, so don't be hard on yourself about this. Instead, what can you do to communicate and demonstrate household stability?

If you don't have a spouse, who else is or could be on your parenting team?

What help can those people give you in creating stability and structure in your home?

Don't Let Your Own Needs Dominate

One last key to building character: *Your own needs aren't the measure* of what's wise to do. For instance, because everybody needs friends, some parents try to make their kids their friends. That's a mistake. Parenting isn't a popularity contest. If you're focused on getting your children to like you, you'll tend to be inconsistent with discipline and household responsibilities. You do need friends, but you need to find friends other than your kids.

Be prepared to insert yourself into areas of life where your children may not welcome your presence. It's okay if they're not thrilled at you for this—again, you're their parent, not their friend. Insert yourself for the right reasons, at the right time, not simply to feel you're in control. If you find yourself getting mad or scared when children push against your control, that's something God will be happy to address with you.

Be willing to make the tough calls—knowing you might antagonize your child. If your natural inclination is to make nice and avoid conflict, go to God with that.

Likewise, go to God with your yearning to raise the doctor or football player that you wanted to become yourself, but didn't. Go to God with your longing for perfection, or your desire to look good in the eyes of other parents. Spend enough time with God that you let Him bring your unmet longings like these to light.

Can you see how much of building a child's character involves building *your* character? The two main reasons why parents back off from revolutionary parenting are:

- They want (or feel compelled) to give their time to other things.

- Their own needs feel so intense that going to God with them doesn't seem like an option, so they try to get their needs met through their kids, or through other things at their kids' expense.

9. Which, if any, of these statements is true of you?

❏   I want my children to see me as a friend.

❏   I don't have close adult friends.

❏   It's important to me that my friends, family, or others think I'm doing a good job as a parent.

❏   I hate not being in control.

❏   It drives me crazy when things in my world aren't perfect.

❏   I don't think I'm good with children.

❏   I hate conflict.

❏   I'm not good at discipline.

❏   I will feel better about myself if my child is successful in a career I have in mind for him or her.

10. If you marked any of the above statements as true, how does that issue affect the way you parent?

11. Every parent has vulnerabilities and imperfections. God is eager to forgive your short-comings and help you grow. Parenting is God-designed to expose those areas of our hearts that aren't fully offered as holy sacrifices to God (Rom. 12:1). What is one of your desires, fears, or things you hate (maybe something you marked as true in question 9) that you want to talk to God about? If you're not yet willing to entrust it to Him, pray that He'll help you become willing to be willing. You can write a prayer here.

12. Which is more important to you: To see your children outperform the other children in their classes, or to see them love the other children in their classes?

13. If asked, would your children say you value character over academic achievement, or vice versa? What would give them that impression?

14. How can you convey to your children what you most value? What can you say? What can you do?

15. As you finish this session, what thoughts and feelings are going through your mind?

For Couples:

➤ Compare your assessments of your children's personalities and character. Do you generally see your children the same way, or do you differ?

➤ Put together your ideas and come up with character traits you want to focus on for each child and steps each of you can take to foster those traits. You might want to write your goals and your first steps for each child on a separate piece of paper. A goal might be: "Nathan: To come to understand what compassion is from God's point of view, why it's important to us as parents, and what it would look like in his life."

➤ By the end of your time with this workbook, you'll want to involve each of your children in setting goals for themselves. Children need to own goals like "grow in compassion" and steps like memorizing verses, and not have such things imposed on them without their understanding of what's going on. How can you begin to involve your children in your planning process? Consider taking time with each of your children individually to start talking with them about the idea of setting goals for their lives.

➤ What would it take for you to structure your family life so that each child gets at least ninety minutes of attention from one of you each day? For instance, maybe you need to tag team so that one of you spends time with one child who currently needs extra attention while the other parent is with the other children. Or maybe one of you needs to take on some household chores to free up the other parent's time to spend with the children. Or maybe you need to take a look at your finances to see where you can trade conspicuous consumption (spending money on stuff) for inconspicuous consumption (sacrificing money and possessions in order to have more time with your family).

➤ It's easy to despair, feeling that parenting is an overwhelming job that we will never be good enough at. It's hard to entrust our needs and our shortcomings to God. Pray Psalm 62 for one another:

My soul finds rest in God alone;
    my salvation comes from him.
He alone is my rock and my salvation;
    he is my fortress, I will never be shaken.

How long will you assault a man?
        Would all of you throw him down—
    this leaning wall, this tottering fence?
They fully intend to topple him
        from his lofty place;
    they take delight in lies.
With their mouths they bless,
        but in their hearts they curse.

Find rest, O my soul, in God alone;
    my hope comes from him.
He alone is my rock and my salvation;
    he is my fortress, I will not be shaken.
My salvation and my honor depend on God;
    he is my mighty rock, my refuge.
Trust in him at all times, O people;
        pour out your hearts to him,
        for God is our refuge.

Lowborn men are but a breath,
    the highborn are but a lie;
if weighed on a balance, they are nothing;

together they are only a breath.
Do not trust in extortion
  or take pride in stolen goods;
though your riches increase,
  do not set your heart on them.

One thing God has spoken,
  two things have I heard:
that you, O God, are strong,
  and that you, O Lord, are loving.
Surely you will reward each person
  according to what he has done.

Pray also for your children, that God will empower them with His Holy Spirit to grow in the character traits you've identified.

notes

DEVELOPING CHARACTER

Open with prayer.

Getting Started

Ask:

> What is one positive character quality you needed today? (For example: honesty, humility, compassion, perseverance.)

Core Concepts

1. Start very young.

2. Use this simple, repetitive process: plan, implement, evaluate, revise, implement.

3. Each child requires a custom process—not one size fits all.

4. Allow development at a pace appropriate to the child.

5. Emphasize character development.

6. Revolutionary Parenting is very hands-on and intense.

7. Parenting is not a popularity contest.

8. Provide structure.

DVD

View part 1 of the DVD segment for session 4. It is called "Intro."

Group Discussion

Some parents will have had a hard time putting words to the goals they have for their children and the concrete steps they can take. If some in your group were able to do this effectively, they can offer their goals and next steps as examples. If all of you find this difficult, see if you can choose one person's child and come up with clearly stated goals and steps for one area in this child's life. Once you get used to thinking in this way, the process becomes easier. Avoid giving each other advice ("these are the goals I think you should have for your child"). Instead, help group members articulate what they want to aim at for their own children.

What are some unpopular things you've had to do in order to help your child develop character?

4. How clear are your children on your household's rules? What evidence do you see of that?

5. Sit down with your children and your new—or reaffirmed—list of rules. (Ideally, do this together with your spouse.) Go over the list with them. Talk about each rule—what it means, why it's important. If the rules are new, explain where you're getting them and why you're suddenly having this meeting. Give your children time to say what they think and ask questions. What pushback, if any, do you get? Do some rules come as news to them, or is the list a no-brainer, given how you've run the household up to now? Are there any rules that surprise them?

6. Ask your kids which of the rules they think are hardest for them to live up to. What do you learn?

Revolutionary Parents told us it was important that the rules were clear, the consequences for breaking them were clear and fit the family's values, consequences were enforced consistently, and they were enforced *without malice*. The approach to discipline varied from family to family (for example, some spanked; others didn't) and even from child to child. But consistency and lack of malice were crucial.

Finding the right blend of freedom and limitations for each unique child is challenging. Some children thrive with more structure, some with less. Some need much firmer discipline when they break a rule than others. Siblings cry, "Unfair!" but we do need to take into account different temperaments and needs as we set boundaries and consequences for each child.

7. What do your children expect will happen if they break your rules?

8. What do you think "without malice" means regarding punishment?

Why is this important?

9. The Revolutionary Parents we talked to said they thought enforcing a curfew was essential for keeping children healthy and helping them develop self-discipline. What do you think about curfews?

What do you see as reasonable curfews for your children, given their ages? Why?

What do you think is a reasonable consequence for your children breaking curfew?

Revolutionary Parents don't hesitate to influence their children's choice of friends, although they do so discreetly—by asking questions and dropping hints rather than (except in extreme cases) forbidding children to see someone. Peers have a huge influence on children, so Revolutionary Parents get to know their kids' peers, spend time with them, and discuss with their children their friends and their friends' habits.

10. Is it important to you to know your kids' friends? Why or why not?

What efforts do you want to put into knowing your children's friends and influencing their choice of friends?

What will it take for you to follow through on those goals?

Media (television, movies, music, Internet, etc.) are another huge influence on children, so Revolutionary Parents monitor, select, and limit their children's media intake. They set clear limits as to what is and isn't appropriate and permissible. They discuss their restrictions with their children and listen to feedback rather than just making pronouncements.

11. What do you think are reasonable limits for each of your children in the following areas?

The amount of television watched per day or per week?

The amount of Internet use (other than schoolwork) per day or per week?

The content of television and movies allowed?

The content of Internet sites?

Use of e-mail, instant messaging, personal web sites, social networking sites (such as Facebook or MySpace) or other forms of your child's Internet presence?

How you should go about supervising what movies and television your children are exposed to?

How you should go about supervising the amount and content of your children's Internet use?

12. Discuss these media ground rules with your spouse and come to agreement. Then sit down with your spouse and each of your children and discuss media rules. Listen to your children's feedback and engage them in dialogue about your reasons for limiting their media intake. Talk with them about the problems embedded in the media content you are restricting. Listen to their opinions, but don't automatically cave in to their demands in order to make them like you. Be willing to take the flak, especially if you've had a highly permissive regime and are now tightening it.

After this meeting, assess: How did it go? What will you do next?

A final area of boundaries to consider has to do with children's activities. They need to learn to work diligently, but wall-to-wall activity hinders the kind of unstructured play, thinking, and even daydreaming that produce adults with rich inner lives and the ability to handle stillness. Overscheduled children grow into activity addicts—adults who can't handle essential spiritual practices like solitude, silence, self-reflection, and self-motivation. If they constantly crave stimulation, how will they have the patience to listen for the still, small voice of God?

13. Are your children overscheduled? What limits do you need to place on their activities? (If it's hard for you to do that, ask yourself what drives you to involve them in so many activities.)

14. At this point, what are your thoughts, feelings, and questions about family rules?

For Couples:

➤ Talk about what rules you think you should set. It's important that you come to agreement so that your children don't get mixed messages about what's expected. If one of you wants to be stricter in some area, talk that through.

➤ Talk about what consequences you think are appropriate for broken rules. Again, listen to each other and work toward consensus.

➤ If you have concerns about your spouse's attitude or behavior, discuss your concerns with kindness. For instance, "I would like you to be firmer [or gentler, or more involved, etc]." If necessary, see a marriage counselor for a few sessions just to help you negotiate ground rules for the household.

➤ Schedule a family meeting to talk about new rules and boundaries. Be prepared for some pushback! You and your spouse need to go into this meeting with agreement so your children can't divide and conquer. At the same time, listen to your children and be willing to make adjustments if necessary. (If you tend to be overly sensitive to your children's approval, then decide ahead of time to err on the side of firmness. If you tend to be a poor listener, then decide ahead of time to err on the side of listening.)

➤ Watch a movie together with your children. Afterward, have a discussion about what was right and wrong with it—both morally and from the viewpoint of spiritual truth. This may seem awkward the first few times you do it, as kids just want to be entertained and not have to think. But they'll get used to thinking critically about media.

➤ Use Psalm 15 as a springboard to pray for your children to grow into adults of strong character:

LORD, who may dwell in your sanctuary?
    Who may live on your holy hill?
He whose walk is blameless
    and who does what is righteous,
who speaks the truth from his heart
    and has no slander on his tongue,
who does his neighbor no wrong
    and casts no slur on his fellowman,
who despises a vile man
    but honors those who fear the LORD,
who keeps his oath
    even when it hurts,
who lends his money without usury
    and does not accept a bribe against the innocent.
He who does these things
    will never be shaken.

▼ notes

DRAWING LINES IN THE SAND

Open with prayer.

Getting Started

Ask:

When you were a child, what was one rule your parents strictly enforced, if any?

Remember (and remind the group if necessary) that these icebreaker questions should not turn into long stories. Answers should take a minute or less.

Core Concepts

1. Identify the parameters by which children must live.

2. Enforce a curfew.

3. Influence their choice of friends.

4. Limit the amount and type of media they consume.

encounter with a stubborn child lights a spark.

Because our words have power to do damage, we have to develop the discipline to control them. Not investing the effort to do this isn't an option. It's an evasion to blame our children when we lose our tempers—if we lack self-discipline, how can we expect it from a child? Also, sometimes children actually make it their goal to get a parent to blow up. It makes them feel powerful or superior. We owe it to them and to God not to fall for such goals that are spiritually harmful to them.

1. How often do you find yourself angry at your children?

2. What do you typically do when you're angry at them?

3. The apostle Paul wrote, "Do not let any unwholesome talk come out of your mouths, but only what is helpful for building others up according to their needs, that it may benefit those who listen" (Eph. 4:29). Would you say the way you deal with your anger builds up your children according to their needs? Explain.

In his epistle, James wrote,

What causes fights and quarrels among you? Don't they come from your desires that battle within you? You want something but don't get it. You kill and covet, but you cannot have what you want. You quarrel and fight. You do not have, because you do not ask God. When you ask, you do not receive, because you ask with wrong motives, that you may spend what you get on your pleasures. (James 4:1–3)

4. James told us that anger usually comes when we want something, don't get it, and instead of taking the disappointment to God, we blow up. Think of a recent time when you were angry at one of your children. What did you want that you didn't get?

What you wanted (perhaps your child's respect) may have been entirely reasonable. But Paul told us not to retaliate for a hurt but to overcome evil with good (Rom. 12:19–21). What a disrespectful child needs is discipline without a vengeful attitude. When we mix in anger from our wounded pride, children may learn to fear us, but they don't learn to respect us. They don't develop character. This is why it's so important to take our unmet desires to God and our friends, and to practice techniques like counting to ten, rather than blowing up.

5. What is one thing you could do to grow in controlling your anger?

Great Parents Have Explainable Reasons

A third behavior of great parents is to have an explainable reason for every decision. Revolutionary Parents go to lengths to explain why they make their choices. They relate their decisions to biblical principles—these are teaching moments. Their consistency of logic and follow-through earns respect, and their willingness to explain their reasoning fosters a deeper relationship with their children.

6. Do you typically have a reason for your decisions that you could explain? Or do you tend to respond to your children by instinct? Describe what you do, and why.

There isn't always time in the heat of the moment to think through our responses. That's why great parents take time outside the heat of the moment to think through a coherent philosophy of right and wrong, family rules, goals for their children, and strategies for getting there. A worldview rooted in biblical principles, which we get by reflecting regularly on the Bible's teachings, offers a coherent framework for decisions. When we know what our rules are and why, then we will usually have a coherent reason for our decisions on the fly.

7. Think about forming a coherent philosophy that would give you consistent reasons for your decisions as a parent and regularly explaining such reasons to your children. What are your thoughts? (Does this approach seem good? Unreasonable? Daunting? Why?)

Great Parents Manage Their Time Efficiently

It's helpful to schedule time with your children, time with God, and so on. In our busy culture, complete spontaneity usually leads us to let important things slide. Instead of being a victim of your schedule, take charge of it. Revolutionary Parents told us there's no such thing as "quality time" with a child without quantity time. Those quality moments emerge when we invest significant amounts of time and attention in our children.

8. What is one step you could take to manage your time better so as to have more time for your children?

Great Parents Listen

Listening is a critical skill for effective parents. We need to listen past our children's words. Most children are not articulate: They often talk about peripherals instead of speaking directly to the issue. We need to ask questions to help them figure out what they mean and communicate it to us. Questions tell children we're listening, show we care, and enable us to hear the message they need to get across.

9. What are your strengths and weaknesses when it comes to listening to your children?

10. What is one thing you could do to listen more effectively? (For example: Turn off the car radio. Make eye contact. Let the child finish before you interrupt. Ask a question that helps a child clarify and doesn't reflect impatience.)

Great Parents Model Important Behaviors

We need to model the important behaviors we want our children to copy. Children naturally do what they see, so modeling is the most influential means of teaching. Three key behaviors we need to model for them are:

1. Love
2. Respect
3. Patience

11. Which of these is the most difficult for you to model when you're with your children? Why do you suppose that's the case?

Great Parents Build Genuine Relationships

Finally, effective parenting is based on a genuine relationship with our kids. A family is about intimate relationships, shared experiences, and moving toward a common goal with deep love and care. Children can tell if we feel love for them and are genuinely committed to their welfare—or if we're just driven to make them turn out a certain way so we can feel good about ourselves. If we pile on the rules without deepening the relationship, children are likely to feel unloved and angry.

In the Bible we see that God offers us both intimate relationship and discipline to help us grow in character. He isn't the cold lawgiver who is strong on rules and weak on relationship. Nor is He the sugar daddy who cuddles us and lets us do what we want. No, He demonstrates costly sacrificial love and calls us to holiness. That's the kind of parent He wants us to be.

Love isn't just warm emotions for our children. Real love translates into time and energy invested in their needs and our relationship with them. When we asked young adults what they felt were the most significant mistakes American parents have made, they said:

1. Failing to provide appropriate discipline.
2. Not spending enough time with their children.

12. How would you describe your relationship with each of your children? (Close? Cool? Stormy? Up and down? Limited by busyness?)

How freely and openly do you communicate with and listen to each of your kids?

How do you let your kids know they matter?

13. Make a plan to spend time with each of your children to deepen your relationship. When will you take time with each one? What will you do together?

For Couples:

➤ Talk about your strengths and weaknesses that this session surfaces. How good at controlling your temper are you? How good a listener are you? If your spouse thinks you have more room for improvement in some area, be willing to hear that constructive critique. (But resist the temptation to lecture your spouse!)

➤ Encourage your spouse about the areas of behavior that are his or her strengths.

➤ Set one or two personal goals for your behavior as a parent. What do you want to improve? How can your spouse support you?

➤ Plan some fun time as a family. How can you communicate love to your children and build stronger relationships?

➤ If one of you has less one-on-one time with the children, how can you juggle your schedules to make time for that? Your children will value getting time alone with the parent who has been less available.

➤ Pray for each other and for your children. You might personalize some of Paul's prayer for his spiritual children in Thessalonica:

Dear brothers and sisters, we can't help but thank God for you, because your faith is flourishing and your love for one another is growing. We proudly tell God's other churches about your endurance and faithfulness in all the persecutions and hardships you are suffering. And God will use this persecution to show his justice and to make you worthy of his Kingdom, for which you are suffering....

So we keep on praying for you, asking our God to enable you to live a life worthy of his call. May he give you the power to accomplish all the good things your faith prompts you to do. Then the name of our Lord Jesus will be honored because of the way you live, and you will be honored along with him. This is all made possible because of the grace of our God and Lord, Jesus Christ. (2 Thess. 1:3–5, 11–12 NLT)

notes

BEHAVING LIKE A PARENT

Open with prayer.

Getting Started

Ask:

What is one thing, good or bad, that you learned about being a parent from your parents?

Core Concepts

1. Fill the parenting role completely and with confidence.

2. Control the temper.

3. Have an explainable purpose for every decision.

4. Manage your time efficiently.

5. Listen.

6. Model important behaviors.

7. Deepen your relationship.

DVD

View part 1 of the DVD segment for session 6. It is called "Intro."

Group Discussion

Are there ways you tend to shy away from being a parent to your child? If so, what are they?

What are some practical ways in which you could improve in your "soft behaviors" with your child—behaviors like temper, listening, philosophy, and consistency?

Encourage every parent to come up with at least one personal goal regarding these behaviors. Some may have trouble setting goals or articulating steps to take, so others can help them by articulating their own goals and steps. You can lead by sharing what you plan to do. You should also take the lead in encouraging parents to follow through on taking action.

3. If you were going to have a conversation with your children about what truth is and where we can go to find it, what might you say?

4. Ask your children to describe their view of God. What's He like? Do you have a picture in your head of how He looks? (At this point you should listen, not correct them.) Afterward, write notes here about what they said.

What do you learn from their answers that can guide you as you become more intentional about training them in Christian faith?

We parents need to make an effort to discuss with our children what truth is and where it comes from (the Bible). We also need to identify for them the nonnegotiables that conflict with what our culture treats as normal. For example, our children need to know that divorce, abortion, homosexual behavior, and promiscuity are simply not okay. When they happen, it's a tragedy. God forgives sin, and we forgive our friends who sin, but that doesn't make these actions okay. The Bible also clashes with our consumer society on issues around money and possessions, success, and the treatment of the poor. Beyond that, it challenges the whole notion that life is about me—my needs, my self-fulfillment, my agenda.

In addition to knowing *what* the Bible says, children need to learn *why* (What rationale does the Bible give for an instruction?) and *so what* (What does this have to do with the purpose and outcome of their lives?).

We can't help our children understand the Bible if we're unfamiliar with it ourselves. But if you're a beginner, don't panic! Simply begin where you are. Most Revolutionary Parents make space in their lives several times a week to read and think about a passage of Scripture. This is how they learn to see situations from a biblical point of view. If you're not already accustomed to doing this, below are six passages from the gospel of Matthew. You can pull out your calendar and schedule three fifteen-minute blocks of time this week and three next week to read and think about each of these passages.

If you care for small children full time, scheduling by the clock may be difficult, so you'll need to be creative. Try turning off the television and other media, and reflect on even a very short passage of Scripture while you fold laundry or wash dishes. Or get an audio Bible to play while you're in the car.

Passages from Matthew for Reflection
(along with some questions to spark your thinking)

The temptations of Christ (Matt. 4:1–11)

What does this set of incidents tell you about Jesus?

What does it reveal about how temptation works?

What does it say about how to overcome temptation?

What do you see here that your children need to know?

Prayer (Matt. 6:5–15)

If prayer isn't meant to impress other people, what's the point of it?

What topics does Jesus' sample prayer (verses 9–13) address?

Which of these topics do you often pray about?

Which do you rarely pray about? Why?

What is one way you could grow in prayer?

What do you see here that would help your children learn to pray?

Judging others (Matt. 7:1–6)

What does Jesus mean by "judging"?

Does Jesus mean there are no standards for assessing the rightness or
wrongness of someone's behavior?

Why is it usually hypocritical to judge what others are doing?

What do you see here that would help your children?

Servanthood (Matt. 20:20–28)

Why would a parent make the request this mother makes of Jesus?

What are your ambitions for your children?

How does Jesus define greatness?

How is this different from the way your world defines greatness?

How easy or hard is it for you to be happy in a servant's role? Why?

What do you see here that your children need to know?

Jesus' crucifixion (Matt. 27:32–56)

Try to make a movie of this scene in your mind. What do you see and hear? What details do you especially notice?

What is Jesus going through at each stage of this scene?

What do you think the women watching this are feeling?

Why is Jesus doing this?

Who is this Jesus in your life?

What difference does He make to your life?

What do you see here that your children need to understand?

Jesus' resurrection (Matt. 27:57—28:15)

Try to make a movie of this set of scenes. What do you see and hear first? Then what?

What details seem especially important to you?

Follow the women throughout these scenes. What do you think they are feeling at each point?

How does Jesus' resurrection affect you and your life?

What do you see here that your children need to know?

Chapter 8 of *Revolutionary Parenting* includes a much longer list of the top Bible passages that Revolutionary Parents told us they thought were important for parents and children to know and embrace. You might want to study each of those passages in turn, and think about how you can start introducing them to your children.

5. What goal(s) do you want to set for your family regarding the Bible? Here are sample goals you could set, along with measurable first steps to get there. Choose or adapt a goal that fits where you are in the process of becoming a Revolutionary Parent, or make up your own goal.

❏ Goal: To learn more about what the Bible says that is relevant to my life and my children's lives. To build Scripture into my life consistently.

Next Step: To do this, I will set aside at least _____ minutes _____ times per week to read and reflect on passages from the Bible. I will do this on these days and times: _____ _____. I will start with this portion of the Bible: _____.

❏ Goal: To make reading and talking about the Bible part of my family's routine.

Next Step: We will read and talk about a passage each week on Thursday nights after dinner. (Choose a day and time that works for you. Chapter 8 of *Revolutionary Parenting* contains a list of Bible passages you could start with. Depending on the ages of your children, you may want to paraphrase the passages or read from a children's Bible.)

❏ My Personal Goal:

My Next Step:

❏ My Family Goal:

My Next Step:

The Church Is Our Support System

In addition to the Bible, the church is a support system every Christian needs. Great parents help their kids: (1) get connected to a spiritual support system, and (2) understand why they need it. Great parents help their children look for friends in a community of faith, because such friends are more likely to have a shared view of what's true and important in life than are friends they meet at school.

We need to treat a faith group as our spiritual family and safety net, so our children will learn to do so too. This means we need to develop and spend time with a true community of faith, not just a bunch of light friendships. Our children need to see us with Christian friends who know us deeper than pleasantries and who care personally about our lives and our faith. They also need to see us contributing our gifts to that community of faith. They need to see us worshipping so they will learn to value worship as part of life.

However, while the church is our support, we can't expect it to play the lead role in cultivating our children's faith. It plays a key role in reinforcing what we teach, but church workers don't have the time one-on-one with our kids they would need to lead in that job. Leadership is our responsibility.

6. Are you currently involved in a church? If so, describe the depth and quality of your relationships there.

7. What help is your church able to offer in reinforcing faith lessons you want your children to learn?

What isn't your church able to do that you need to do?

8. Perhaps your church has disappointed your search for support. You may even have stopped going to church. But think about your need for real friends who support your growth in Christ, and your children's need for friends and a faith community that reinforce their faith. What goal do you want to set regarding your own need for support?

❏ My Personal Goal:

What goal will you set regarding your children's need for a church that reinforces their faith?

❏   My Goal for My Children:

What action will you take to begin to address those goals?

Servanthood Should Be a Lifestyle

In addition to reading the Bible with their children and taking them to church, Revolutionary Parents also train their children to be servants by giving them opportunities to serve both with the family and on their own. Such parents set an example by volunteering at homeless shelters, food pantries, or other ministries to those in need, and they involve their children in those efforts. They take a child with them when they go to an elderly person's home to do repair work, or they send a child to mow the elder's lawn.

We may feel we and our children are too busy to do some act of service at least once a month. Here we bump up once more against priorities: Is it more important to us that our children learn to be great soccer players or great servants? Children will only give lip service to Christ's example of servanthood unless parents instill it as a habit that is as important as finishing one's homework. After each act of service, Revolutionary Parents debrief the experience with the child to underscore lessons learned.

9. What obstacles do you face in making service at least a monthly habit for yourself and your children? (Talk about both practical obstacles, like time, and also any emotional obstacles you face.)

10. You've already set several goals for yourself in this session, so maybe service feels like something that could safely wait for another day. But take a few minutes to think about it anyway. How could you start building service into your own life? Maybe your church has ministries to the poor, the homeless, unwed mothers, and so on. Your community newsletter may also have volunteer opportunities. What could you do even for one hour a month?

How could you start building service into your children's lives? (For instance, can they join you in a church-run ministry to the needy? Is there something kind they could do for a classmate? An elderly neighbor?)

Prayer Is Essential

Prayer is another essential value to build into your own life and your children's. Revolutionary Parents talk with God often about their dreams for and concerns about their children. They know that seeing their children come to faith in Christ is of eternal importance, so they do everything they can to provide the knowledge and motivation for their children to make that commitment. But instead of pressuring children to pray a prayer of faith, Revolutionary Parents told us they prayed for years for their children, asking God to draw them to Him, knowing that a conversion in response to a parent's pressure may not be real enough to last.

Revolutionary Parents also make themselves available to hear God's response to their prayers as they read the Scriptures. They practice the skill of silent meditation, listening for God's still, small voice. And they pray with their children at least daily, encouraging them to thank God and to pray when making critical decisions.

11. When can you pray with your children? Make a list of opportunities you have. (At breakfast? In the car? At dinner? Before bed?)

12. When can you pray on your own?

Love Is the Centerpiece

The Bible, the church, service, prayer—these are all crucial elements to build into our own lives and our children's lives. And amid all of these, love is the centerpiece of the Christian life. To model God's love for us, we provide our children with unconditional love—we treat them with affection and care no matter what they do. We are involved with our children each day and watch for times and ways to express love to them. We soften their nature without breaking their spirit, seeking to minister to them with gentleness, humility, vulnerability, and kindness.

Reading the Bible with the family, praying together, and especially doing acts of service aren't fun for many kids. If we enforce these practices without surrounding them with an environment of unconditional love, children will likely learn that Christian faith is about dry duty and performance. But if we consistently communicate love through word and action, they may squawk about having to mow the neighbor's lawn or talk about the Bible instead of watching television, but they'll grow into adults who know that love is at the heart of all God asks of us.

We can think of these values—the Bible, the church, service, prayer, and love—as a healthy family diet. These aren't activities to check off a list, but habits to build into our families on a consistent basis. Some of us are crash dieters who jump into a drastic regimen but quickly burn out. By contrast, what our children really need is for us to build up these nourishing habits over time and stick with them for the long haul.

13. What can you do this week to let your children know you love them?

14. You've been sketching out goals and action steps regarding the Bible, the church, service, prayer, and love. That's a lot to absorb if several of these aren't already part of the fabric of your busy life. What are you thinking and feeling about all of this?

For Couples:

➤ Talk about where you want the Bible, the church, service, and prayer to fit into your lives and your children's lives. Talk honestly about the obstacles you see, but also about the benefits. Together, try to set a goal in each of these areas. How can you support each other in building these into your family?

➤ Discuss how you communicate unconditional love to your children. How are you doing with helping each other have time with the children?

➤ Plan time with each of your children individually to talk about the things that are changing in your home. Listen to them.

➤ Plan a family meeting to talk about what is changing in your family.

➤ Pray for your children's salvation. Pray also for discernment about the goals you're setting. You might want to personalize this prayer of Paul's:

I have not stopped thanking God for you. I pray for you constantly, asking God, the glorious Father of our Lord Jesus Christ, to give you spiritual wisdom and insight so that you might grow in your knowledge of God. I pray that your hearts will be flooded with light so that you can understand the confident hope he has given to those he called—his holy people who are his rich and glorious inheritance.

I also pray that you will understand the incredible greatness of God's power for us who believe him. This is the same mighty power that raised Christ from the dead and seated him in the place of honor at God's right hand in the heavenly realms. (Eph. 1:16–20 NLT)

6. Serve others in order to grow.

7. Speak with God often.

DVD

View part 1 of the DVD segment for session 7. It is called "Intro."

Group Discussion

By this time the group should be ready to go straight to discussing goals. But if you get pushback, step back and discuss why it's important to have goals in each of these four areas: Bible, church, service, and prayer. Remind the group not to tell each other what their goals should be. Ask parents (or couples) to share their own goals and perhaps talk about why they chose those goals.

How are you helping your children "catch" faith, rather than just teaching it to them?

What has changed in how you demonstrate faith to your children since session 3?

What else can you do to help your children catch faith? What goals and steps did you write in the workbook?

What are some practical ways you can use available tools (such as the Bible, church, mission trips, and service) to help develop your child's faith? What goals and next steps did you come up with as you did the workbook exercises?

What obstacles will you have to deal with in order to follow through on those steps?

DVD

View part 2 of the DVD for session 7 now. It is called "Review." After viewing the video, take a few minutes to discuss any questions the video raises about what your group has discussed in this lesson. Then move on to your prayer time.

Prayer

Ask, "How can the group pray for you as a parent?"

Pray Ephesians 1:16–20 for each other and for your children.

LEANING ON GOD

IN THE PREVIOUS SEVEN SESSIONS, you've assessed your family and started setting goals in a wide range of areas. Now it's time to pull all that together into a coherent plan that is manageable for you. Let's start with the big picture and then zero in on the details.

As you proceed with this process, think of yourself as your children's *coach*. Not as their best friend. Not as a dictator. You're a coach, training your children to be the best they can be at the sport called Life. You need a game plan—goals and a strategy for reaching those goals.

As you create this first draft of your plan, it's important to turn to God with worship and a request for help. The biblical writers have some important perspectives on planning:

> *Mortals make elaborate plans,*
> > *but God has the last word.*
>
> *Humans are satisfied with whatever looks good;*
> > *God probes for what is good.*
>
> *Put God in charge of your work,*
> > *then what you've planned will take place. (Prov. 16:1–3 msg)*
>
> *Look here, you who say, "Today or tomorrow we are going to a certain town and will stay there a year. We will do business there and make a profit." How do you know what your life will be like tomorrow? Your life is like the morning fog—it's here a little while, then it's gone. What you ought to say is, "If the Lord wants us to, we will live and do this or that." Otherwise you are boasting about your own plans, and all such boasting is evil. (James 4:13–16 nlt)*

The message here is not that planning is bad, but that good planning requires genuine reliance on God. So take a moment now to pray, perhaps along these lines:

Lord, here I am. I offer myself to you as Your servant. You are the Lord of plans, the Creator of my children and me. Thank You for entrusting them to me as Your gift. Whatever I do today in my planning, and whatever I do as a parent, I want to do it in You. I don't want to do it in my own power, for my own glory. My truest identity is as Your child. What are You doing in my children's lives, and how can I help? What do You want them to become and do? What do You want me to become and do?

1. Start with *vision*. What is the job of a Christian parent, as you understand it?

2. How deeply invested are you in your identity as a Christian parent, and in the parenting process? How devoted are you to being the best, most biblical parent you can be?

3. By now you have some idea of the cost and benefit of making God your top priority and parenting your top area of ministry. What adjustments to your life are you willing to make?

4. Are there any adjustments you are *not* willing to make? If so, what are they and why?

5. What are the central values and beliefs you want to instill in your children?

6. Try to put into words up to six *life goals* you have for each of your children. (Look back at sessions 1 and 2, as well as what you observed in session 4 about each child's strengths and weaknesses.) As you formulate life goals, ask yourself, "Am I seeking to form these children into my image, or God's?"

Name:

1.

2.

3.

4.

5.

6.

Name:

1.

2.

3.

4.

5.

6.

Name:

1.

2.

3.

4.

5.

6.

7. Look back at what you wrote in sessions 4 through 7, and pull together here all your goals for yourself and for each of your children. Most of these will be short- and medium-term goals, things you want to build into your life and your family over the next year or so.

Goals for me (my spiritual life, my behavior, my habits, things I want to model for my children, and so on):

(Examples: Let my children know I love them. Establish consistent household rules. Follow through on rules and expectations I've established, with consistent consequences for breaking the rules. Grow more courageous and loving in dealing with conflict with my children.)

Goals for my spouse and me as a couple:

(Examples: Communicate every day about the kids and our parenting. Talk about how we're doing with our goals and what needs to be done. Encourage each other. Demonstrate that we are committed to each other for the long haul.)

Goals for my child [name] _____:

(Consider character traits to develop, habits to build, household chores to take on. Involve your child in the process of setting these goals. Share your thoughts, ask your child for feedback, and listen. Remember, though, that parenting isn't a democracy, and your child doesn't get to veto all attempts to set goals.)

Goals for [name] _____:

Goals for [name] _____:

8. What steps do you need to take to reach these goals? (Focus first on your steps for the next month or two. Then include longer-term steps.)

9. What steps does each of your children need to take?

Name:

Name:

Name:

10. Now pull together a list of the top rules or boundaries you want to set for your family. These may be different for different children, depending on their ages and needs (see session 5). With each boundary, describe what you will do to enforce it, and the consequence you will set if a child violates it.

11. How will you make sure your children understand these boundaries?

LEANING ON GOD

Open with prayer. You might use or adapt the prayer in this chapter of the workbook.

Getting Started

Ask:

> How are you feeling right now about the planning process you have been working through?

Core Concepts

1. You are a coach; be the best.

2. Being a godly parent is your primary job at this point in life.

3. Approach the job intelligently and aggressively.

4. You cannot give what you don't have; make sure you're ready.

5. Communicate effectively.

6. Always rely upon God for strength and wisdom.

7. You may do everything "right" and still not produce a spiritual champion.

8. Your child—and the effort you pour into parenting—is your greatest legacy.

DVD

View part 1 of the DVD segment for session 8. It is called "Intro."

Group Discussion

Choose two of the life goals you wrote down for your children (workbook question 6) and discuss why they're important to you.

How will you coach them to reach those life goals?

How are you demonstrating these life goals in your own life?

Where are you right now regarding the costs of making your children this high a priority in your life? What adjustments to your life is this calling from you, and how committed are you to making those adjustments? Why?

How has this group helped you?

How can we continue to help you?

You may find that parents are only beginning to pull together a plan for raising their children and would like the ongoing support of meeting once or twice a month. You'll implement, evaluate, and revise your plans as you go along, so it may be helpful to check in with others periodically to see what they've done and how they have revised their plans.

DVD

View part 2 and 3 of the DVD for session 8 now, called "Review" and "Conclusion." They contain a few more questions and some final words of encouragement.

Prayer

Pray for each group member individually. Allow time for the others to thank God for something they have gained from having that person in the group. Pray for them as parents and for their children.

You have a plan! Not a perfect plan set in stone, but a place to begin. You'll want to revisit this plan within the next thirty days to make adjustments. But don't give up if it doesn't all work out perfectly right away! Plan to make more adjustments in sixty days, and after that revisit your plan at least every three months for the first year.

Every six months, go through your goals and assess how you and your children are doing. By the time they're around seven years old, involve them in the process of evaluating how they're doing and setting (or renewing) their goals. It will be important not to send the message that you love them more if they have performed well. You don't want to raise anxious, performance-driven approval seekers. Avoiding this will require that you give them plenty of unconditional love before, during, and after the goal-setting and evaluation process. Goals are valuable, but children also need space just to be children.

Try not to focus on the daily ups and downs. With faith and character formation, it's essential to take the long view. It may take ten or fifteen years to see your stubborn child show real patience, or your self-focused child develop compassion, or your child who rolls her eyes at church come to enthusiastic faith in Christ. Until they're adults, children likely won't appreciate boundaries, family Bible study, service projects, or discipline.

Finally, remember that sometimes parents do everything "right" and their children grow up indifferent to God. Even God said about Israel, "the children I raised and cared for have rebelled against me" (Isa. 1:2 NLT). If even God—the perfect Parent—raised rebellious children, it might happen to you despite your best efforts. Children have free will, and there is a spiritual battle for their hearts. Parents are not the only influence on them.

Results, therefore, are up to God. Your part is to be faithful and trust Him, knowing that He wants good for your children even more than you do. May your children grow to be adults who love God passionately, care for their neighbors, and train their children to do the same.

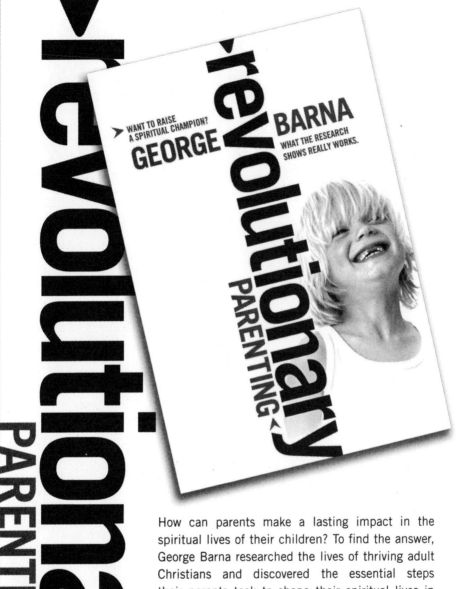

How can parents make a lasting impact in the spiritual lives of their children? To find the answer, George Barna researched the lives of thriving adult Christians and discovered the essential steps their parents took to shape their spiritual lives in childhood. He also learned surprising truths about which popular parenting tactics just aren't working. *Revolutionary Parenting* goes beyond youth group and Sunday school and shows parents how to instill in their children a vibrant commitment to Christ.

CP0289